MW01532661

FOREWARD:

Hello, my valued readers. My name is Jason Burke, and despite being published in a ton of places prior, this is my first foray into publishing my very own book. In this poetry compilation, I explore many relatable and controversial issues that I hope you'll all enjoy. I've always relished the idea of writing a foreward for my own book, but now that I have the chance, it's not as easy as I'd hoped. First off, I suppose I should explain that I've always loved writing, even as a child. I'd create books and scripts in my room at the ripe age of 7, and while the books may not have gotten any better, I'm still at it today. This particular project has taken years. Not because I didn't have the drive or the content, but because I'm a perfectionist who is never sure his work is ready for the public. I write not only as an escape and an outlet for myself, but for others as well. My hope is to provide clarity, or to say things others have needed to hear, but never been able to say to themselves. Enjoy my ramblings as I tackle things like: my disability, childhood, vacations, love, loss, faith, careers, comedy, friends and life lessons. Hopefully these will give you an insight into the type of person I am, as I long to have a personal relationship with my readers. This book skips around from free-verse to rhyming, happy to sad, and silly to serious, so you can pick it up and put it down when you please. I've included little *Afterthoughts* after each poem, to give you a little more insight on where I was coming from as I wrote each piece. I'm a word-nerd, so please bear with my large vocabulary and descriptions. Well just like in life, I'm "talking" too much here, so I'd better get to the thank-you's. First off, thank you to my God, my Lord Jesus for saving me. I've had more blessings in life than anyone could ever ask for, and it ALL comes from Him. Thank you to all of you, my friends, family, and poetry supporters who are buying and reading this book. I couldn't do any of this without you. I appreciate every single one of you. Thank you to my parents, for giving me a wonderful childhood, whose memories are scattered all throughout these pages. They made me into a man who is proud of his life so far. "Never Say Goodbye" is named after a great lesson my mother taught me, before she passed away a few years ago. She wrote as a child, and always hoped/wanted me to be a writer as well. So if you don't like this book, you can blame her. *laughs* Just kidding, she'd kill me for saying that. Mom, thanks for being so supportive and being the namesake of this compilation. Thanks to my "Meemaw" for being one of the best people I know. Thanks to my aunts, uncles, and cousins for being so closely embedded in my life as a youngster, and always treating me like a good man. Thanks to my DCS family, my Wilson family, and my CCAC family. Thanks to my Duquesne churches, pastors, and everyone who has helped with my charity foundations. Thanks to everyone who read some of these poems on Facebook and Twitter, and encouraged/asked me to continue. So I think I've babbled enough here, I'm going to let you get to the poetry now. I hope I get the chance to do another one of these books, but if I don't, I'm proud of this one, and I think it's the biggest part of my legacy thus far. I hope you all enjoy and share these poems, and read them often. If I can make just one of you feel better by reading them, I've done my job. Love yourselves, and love each other…

ESCAPE TO FOREVER:

As I sit at our table, another wave crashes.
So I felt motivated to create you this passage.
The visions surround you, the smells roam your
mind, the moments that matter most, stand alone for
all time.
Extravagant memories, placating your brain.
The thoughts of them fading, too scary to face.
Comparisons useless, no experience ever,
synonymous with hotels extending forever.
The shoreline a painting, the stores an exhibit,
the water is endless, the options infinite.
The planes overhead, delivering sales.
The roaring wind lofting, leaving no trail.
The boards and umbrellas, giving illusions of flight,
and looks from the people, passing into the night.
You peer at the distance, each building the tallest,
with seashells and moonlight providing the solace.
Descriptions of places that can't be defeated,
but words would injustice what can't be repeated.
I don't mean to minimize something so grand,
I just filter the words to make those understand.
Escapism common, the beach lends compassion,
to every infraction with every attraction.
I don't mean for this to sound too analyzed,
but Myrtle's the heaven among hell's disguised.
The smell of the lotion and sand all around,
is simply the greatest, no need to expound.
The wind on your back, the hot air sensation,
as I sit near the beach, which provides inspiration.
So now I will go off, create demonstration,
but I expect for these words to provide inclination.

Afterthought: I wanted to start this book off with

something positive, and "ESCAPE TO FOREVER" seemed perfect, since I want this book to be an escape from the stresses of life. Since Myrtle Beach is like a second home to me and a huge part of my families life, I have a collection of poems I've written from there, and this one paints the best picture of it.

IF I WROTE A NOTE TO YOU:

If I wrote a note to you,
here's what it would say.
As happy as I am with life,
I can't help but complain.

I thank you for your company,
though I can't help but analyze,
if our bond is tight and true,
or you're wearing a disguise.

There's days that I'm the only one,
and days I feel I'm last,
when it comes to your trust and vision,
because I can't trust my past.

If I wrote a note to you,
I'd say I'm only on one track.
But you have to work with people,
because you won't get these days back.

If I wrote a note to you,
I'd hide it on an inner shelf.
If you can't trust those around you,
How can you trust yourself?

Afterthought: You're going to notice a lot of unified themes in this book. The strongest of which, may be friendship. I spent a lot of my formative years wondering what others thought of me, and struggling with the idea that friends come and go. This one is a short piece written long ago, --one of many in this book--, exploring the uncertainty of the ups and downs in close friendships.

THOUGHTS 12 HOURS FROM HOME:

As he crossed the state boundary he thought,
no I'm never going home.
To the doctors and the disappointed family,
and the feeling of being alone.
He thought about his shortened lifespan,
his lonely house in disarray.
The pressure building and expanding,
makes it easy just to float away.

As he lay on the beach there he thought,
he should dig a hole and disappear.
As the town at home sees massive potential,
he sees death closing in every year.
He thought about the ones he'd loved and lost,
and the ones that stuck around.
The broken family name he carries on his back,
how could he ever let them down?

As he sat by the pool room he thought,
why did God keep me here?
He could have chosen so many others,
the message is so unclear.
He thought he was lucky to have this condition,
he'd never take a second back.
But every night he lies awake wondering,

what if he falls flat?

As he paced on the boardwalk he thought,
maybe I should just stay.
I'll delete Facebook and turn off my phone,
would they even care anyway?
He thought about the years spent fighting,
the surgeries putting it all at stake.
Why not start a new life here?
There's only so many times your heart can break.

As he sat in the condo he thought,
this was not like him now.
Negativity and sadness burning his spirit,
he had to bring back the love somehow.
He thought about keeping the language brief,
as his heart hit a rough palpitation.
No need for big words or a flow this time,
the message would be lost in translation.

As he stood on the balcony he thought,
I could never take this leap.
I've still got too much to prove there,
as another car flies down the street.
He thought about the things he had done well,
like basketball, friends, and the stage.
The negative sadness must come to an end,
so he's going back to that place.

As he sat in the car there he thought,
I can't wait to get home.
These broken legs have fight left in them,
and this life has a long way to go.
He realized this as another test,
that God has sent down below.
But he will get through it, stronger than ever,

and he's only 12 hours from home.

Afterthought: This is one of my most emotional and powerful pieces, in my humble opinion. This is another from the Myrtle Collection. This is also the first in a few selections where I talk about my disability. This encompasses the inner struggle between desperately wanting to make an impact in my short time on this earth, and every person's fear that they may not be good enough. Most importantly, it ends on a positive note, because love must always win the battle with hate.

THE BIRD I'VE SWALLOWED:

One eye opens, the light and weight of the day beseech me. The blinding crises pulls my desolate body from my cave, showing me the many ways to aggravation. Though that feeling is only temporary. For all demeaning moments last but seconds in a day, and spirits are what turns them to hours. I look out my broken window, and I bask in the air between two clouds, I see what the birds see, what we should all see. My vision expands infinitely, and I feel empowered in my childish idiocy. The sun will always rise as the wave will always break. The nature to want to fly is always more telling than the eventual landing. The bird I've now swallowed walks the runway of my crowded mind, pecking away at the boulders, and leaving more space for those clouds.

Afterthought: Finally I've shown you that I don't rhyme in every single poem. This one is meant to show how much beauty there is in the world, and how important it is to have perspective. Our problems have a way of holding us hostage, but in reality, the best times in life occur when we notice our blessings and realize that tomorrow is always a new day.

LIGHTHOUSE:

For a long period in my self-sabotaging life, I was surrounded in darkness. All the pains of being me stood on top of a mountain I was too afraid to climb. Every step forward logged another pothole in my attempt to get to stable ground. As good as my inside was, the outside was clouded, hardened by one bad call or another. Rowing in a boat that never goes anywhere but in circles can be the most tiring thing on the planet. But then, finally, I fixed my gaze upon your lighthouse. Your bubbly personality shone through and cast a beam onto my troubles. Your multi-talented, uber-kind towers provided rest, clarity and an escape from always having to be a captain of a sinking ship. You showed me a beauty that wasn't about attraction or contingency. And though my eyes can't always find those towers these days, your illumination continues to touch every traveler that has the graces to find you. As your lighthouse and my boat may drift in opposite directions, I can never forget or repay those nights of becoming whole again. I want to return there some day, and steer others into the beauty of that direction.

Afterthought: This is another in the close personal friends series. The person this was written about, I don't believe, has ever seen this poem. I wrote it long ago, and modified it as circumstances changed. Sometimes friendships can change overnight, people can simply grow apart. But that doesn't change the bond or memories. And this person deserves to know her impact and constant kindness with forever stay with me. I hope she's reading this, and I hope it finds her well. She'll know it belongs to her when she sees it.

THE LONGEST DAY:

Another long morning. I wake up in a drowsy heap because the garbage truck outside decides that 5AM is a good time to pick up garbage. Why do all garbage trucks have to sound like the Incredible Hulk is eating a small village? My mind embodies a Mobius script that runs with the 30 million things I have to get done in the next 6 hours. As I go to shower and put on that first pot of coffee, I realize that the worst thing about morning is the way the light seems to want to kill you as it attacks your eyes. Now I have to trudge along to a meeting to listen to people I don't care about, talk about things that don't affect me. Fun! After that's over, I sit and wait on my Access ride, which is undoubtedly going to take an extra half hour, just to piss me off. After riding around, listening to people who make the Golden Girls look like the Spice Girls, banter about cats named Gertrude and Thelma, I arrive home just in time to see that the gas company has made an error on my bill. Now I have the privilege of sitting on the phone, listening to 37 mid-tempo saxophone ballads, just so I can get finally get through to a guy who doesn't understand English. But first, I have to get through the 18 menu options and punch in my 22 digit account number 3 times. Once I lose that argument, it's time for comestibles. But the pizza place I like doesn't deliver here, because they heard there was a shooting here in 1947. Oh well, there's always Ramen noodles. But I finally get to do something I enjoy, because I'm going to compose a new poem for the Sphinx Cafe tonight. And the title is....oh crap, the dryer just broke. Might as well chuck $400 out the window right now. Like a heat seeking missile, 4 friends text me simultaneously so we can go out and air out our girl problems. Oh, can we please go to the place that has $9 beers?! Yes! I get home and my body is in pain. Guess it's raining outside, and I didn't drink enough. Now I can't even watch my sports in peace. It doesn't matter, because the Pirates are never going to the playoffs anyway. Not that I can focus on anything regardless, because the 13 kids outside are beating my fence with a stick, and there isn't a parent in sight. Meanwhile, this poem is stupid, because nothing even rhymes and that's all I'm good at. Guess it's time for bed, because I love my 2 hours of sleep per night. Oops, here comes that garbage truck again…

Afterthought: One of my other professions is being a stand-up comedian. So I modified a few of my stand-up bits and made them into comedic poems. A lot of my poetry is heavy and deep, so I included a few sarcastic and self-deprecating pieces like this to show another side of myself. Everyone has days like this, and it's better to laugh at them than to let them upset you.

FREE FALL:

Saturday's perfection, but Sunday's a chore,
every time I change colors in your eyes.
Our intimate moments could mean so much more,

but I need to pull truth from the lies.

I feel like I'm crying wolf, grasping at straws,
but I'm squinting beyond the illusion.
I find sweet contentment in learning your flaws,
then you go and change the conclusion.

So I'm shouting your name, at the top of my lungs,
from my roof, for no one to hear.
The tree fell in the forest, not making a sound.
Our vessel sits docked at the pier.
So lets make an escape, put all this behind us,
move forward, uncover it all,
Can I stay on this roof, seeing what no one sees,
or am I set to take a free fall?

My mind gets no rest, from losing this game,
as your bubble gets filled with perception.
You want them to see you igniting the flame,
but all you show me is redemption.

I procure these investments because I see me,
a mirror, with cracks in it's frame.
The facts lay in common and souls intervene,
our shelled hearts both soften the same.

So I'm shouting your name, as loud as I can,
from my roof, but I'm all alone.
It's like you're a ghost that nobody can feel,
silence at the end of the phone.
So let's make an escape, to the top of the world,
live like king and queen, servants and all.
Shall I sit up high for you, lighting the night,
or am I gonna take a free fall?

So I'm shouting your name, until my voice fades,

from the stars, but it's lonely up here.
The air's getting thinner, my heart has grown weary,
your 'character' drowns me in fear.
So lets make an escape, become just one person,
or quiet me, once and for all.
Unveil to the world what I've known all along,
or push me into the free fall.

Afterthought: Everyone has that one friend/partner
that nobody can understand why you like them.
Those people that show you every bit of
themselves, but hide or turn to stone in front of the
rest of the world. This was my attempt at showing
everyone that consistency is important, and
everyone deserves to see your goodness and light
without judgment.

BULLETPROOF:

Certain moments pop up in every persons life that
let them know that fate and destiny do exist. That
somehow among all the dark times that go along
with growing up, God shines that light down on us
to brighten those days with his surreal coincidences
that change us forever. Never was this more evident
than the day your blinding light exploded through
those theatre doors for the first time. Beyond that
inviting smile and compacted infectious energy,
none of my dark clouds ever stood a chance. None
of the incessant problems of college life seemed to
matter in the presence of your sweet spirit.
Everything you touched turned to encouraging
shades of blue instead of the normal gray. Your toes
touching a dance Marley provided a step into the
stars for the world as it watched you shine, and we
simply felt lucky to be a part of the music. We

shared a stage together, and in a time that is meant to be as stressful as any, your open arms made me feel more at home than any other four walls ever have. Your elevating words provided a crutch as I tripped through rough times, and your actions inferred you like the wind, always there, even when one loses sight of it. Your physical frame may have preceded you, but your heart has always been exponentially bigger than your body. What you've overcome makes you ten feet tall and bulletproof, and growing more everyday. Now God has called you to a new area, to carry that light inside you and let it loose on another lucky barrage of unsuspecting cynics. Their lives, too will change, and their clouds, too will fade away inside the heaven that you bring to Florida. So keep these words close when your clouds seem to be relentless, and know that no amount of distance will ever make you alone. As you chase your dreams and continue to bounce the bullets of others away with your amazing talents, recall in the best and worst of times, that you have a friendship here that's ten feet tall and bulletproof.

Afterthought: There are very few poems I write that are composed with one specific person in mind. This one was written for a good friend of mine who was about to move away, as I wanted to leave her some poignant words of encouragement and let her know what she's meant to me. While I won't name her specifically, I want to thank her for letting me include this piece in my book.

TOMBSTONE:

What I never got to say, was 'I'm sorry'. Sorry for

the plight in my defense, sorry for the
Times that I lost, sorry for the times I was so sorry
that I lost. My imperfect perfectionism left your
breath so short, and times I played the role and
turned your hearts into my sport. What I never got
to say, was 'I made it'. I moved so many mountains
on this journey, yet I always feared to revel. The
pressures of the rain kept my attitude from lifting
against the sky. Nobody likes a showoff, and
nobody likes to be unliked. What I never got to say,
was 'I need you'. No matter what the day, your lack
of presence kept me incomplete, at my own behest.
Just know that it was different in our case. Every
day. I step back to read this tombstone, the
inscription makes me proud, the way I've lived for
others, holds this silence screaming loud. This life is
but a minute, but please celebrate this day, now that
I've finally said what I never got to say.

Afterthought: This was a workshop poem that I
created with one of my best friends. At the time,
these were a few regrets I'd had and things I'd kept
in my subconscious. The purpose was to always
keep your slate clean, and never left anything
unsaid. If you were to die tomorrow, make sure
your mind is clear today.

SNOW DAY:

Every other day,
you were the one to walk away.
The true fruits of success were never really tasted,
the anguish near obsession, obliterated, wasted.
After months of communication, I hung my soul on
the connection, yet even battle tested, it somehow
got infected. Should I again blame myself for

another slipping anchor, or even worse, turn my bitter feelings into anger? The pattern yet continues, the more I get invested, and end up on the losing end, like a trembling adolescent.

But this time I choose moving forward, going through the process. As much as it pains me to lose another, I can't forego my progress. Big things are on the horizon now, as I gain exposure, so these words on a page amount to a lot, especially in closure. Your heart is golden, this I know, you'll always have my support, you'll do great things, but in my eyes, you've finally fallen short.

Where we went wrong, where we lost, it seems I'll never know, but now for months, I've been holding on, while you've been letting go. Now the roles are reversed, a lifted curse, my skies turn to blue from gray, when it comes to you, I never knew, and never thought I'd say, I'm breaking away, rising above, and taking a snow day.

Afterthought: At some point in your life, every person has some relationship where they're more invested than the other person is. Where they feel toyed with and taken advantage of, used and confused. This is a piece that may shed light and provide closure to those relationships. Some people can't be changed, saved, or convinced. You have to put yourself first sometimes, no matter how much it hurts.

THE ONE THAT HASN'T GOTTEN AWAY YET:

It's funny that I see you every day and still don't

know your name. I have no idea what you
look like, just a punctured fleeting image in my
shallow mind. As unknown as you are to me,
you're the reason I'm alive. My better half that
hasn't yet completed me. The proof that I was
always wrong, the proof that love exists. Your ideal
is the drive behind the masses and the all-inclusive
search that powers our inconsistent flesh. Take my
sinking boat and all my imperfections, and find me
a dock inside your warmth to call my home. Change
everything I've known and reaffirm my path to
greatest existence. Take away my misconceptions
and provide me growth and adolescence. Hit me
when I least expect it but most need it. Make my
insecurities disappear like mirages in the sweltering
desert heat. Let me forget the ones before you, and
remember lifetimes after you. Make everyday our
first date and every night a resolution from the
intrepid hustle of tedious life. You're either my
solace, or a ghost inside the haunting walls of my
mind. A piece of my noble heart, or the death of my
inner hero. Please let me be wrong, let me find you.
My waiting ears can't stand to hear the deadly echo
of talking to myself.

Afterthought: This was another of those workshop
poems, and the idea this time was to write to the
current love of your life. I didn't have one at that
time, so I liked the idea of writing to my future
better half. I'm quite the romantic at heart.

SHARING WORDS WITH GOD:

Dear God,

If I wrote a note to you,

Here's what it would say,
I'm striving for perfection,
But need help along the way.
The pathway glistens brightly,
And I know I'll be OK,
But bestow upon me wisdom,
And pull me through the fray.

If I passed you in the halls Lord,
I'd thank you for the chance,
They said I'd never make it,
But you provided the advance.
I don't know why You did it,
And I suppose I never will,
But I'll work for You each day,
To turn my luck to skill.

If I saw you sitting near me God,
I'd ask what will impend,
Though this movie thing is working out
And I'm blessed to have my friends.
This life You saved is going well,
It gets hard to believe,
But I can't take a second off,
There's too much I've yet to achieve.

If I crossed you on the street, my Lord,
I'd ask how much more I can do,
I have this need to save them all,
And try to be like You.
For some reason, I'm loved here,
So it must be a success,
But yet I feel I'm falling short,
Please put my mind to rest.

If we could share some tears God,

I'd hope You'd be impressed,
I have to aid this world You made,
By ripping off my vest.
As lucky as I am though,
I feel I must confess,
I give and love with all my heart,
Make them see it, and invest.

When we're face to face in heaven, Lord,
I'll hope I've made you proud,
My eyes still beam and my heart screams,
My feelings like a child.
I had to write these words to You,
As they stuck in my throat,
But now they all know how I feel,
So I can put away my note.

Afterthought: Right off the bat, I know religion is a
hot-button issue, and will turn some people off to
this poem. But my goal here was to get people to
really know who I am, and one of the most
important aspects of my life is my Faith and
Christianity. No matter what your denomination or
belief is, the idea of writing a note to that person is
pretty cool. It's a short way of detailing my life's
mission to help others and hope I'm succeeding on
Earth.

LUCIDITY:

Falling off the grid is a rush more empowering than
any broken wave or Parasailing trip. The ability to
absolve yourself and leave things up to uncontested
winds is one I never gained until I left the mainland.
I was so used to filling up my bucket full of tears
that I never stopped to think of how I'd react when it

overflowed. But in this quiet night's escape I see that trying to force a change is impossible, for it doesn't come naturally. Once the sun sets on tomorrow, everything goes back to the way it was, with this beach and all it's memories as mere fading pictures that dull over time. So as this saving respite comes to its close, I see it for what it is, and hope that this feeling of freedom and peace and come visit me from time to time, providing momentary tranquility in between the dunes of reality.

Afterthought: Another from the beach collection. I love poems that let you escape your problems and rest your spirit. This was written the night before I left the beach for the final time (so far). Read these types of poems when the cold or the bills or the laundry start to pile up.

FALSE FATALITY:

Spending years at a time along for the ride,
As you bring out the worst from inside me.
Every time that you leave with a trail full of lies,
I continue to follow you blindly.
You inflate my ego with the emptiest words,
And I hang on to your every sentence.
My hopes start to rise like a flock full of birds
And you move to the next, no repentance

The truth is, I'd rather be hated in truth,
Than loved by emotion that's false.
Which is why I stay guarded, consorted in youth,
Forge to maintain a consistent pulse.
Don't feed me words that you don't really mean,
That's as simple as I can explain,
My own paranoia has kept me so green,

This heart gets so hard to maintain.

My friendships' important, my actions proficient
It means less to you, I can tell.
Everyone leaves, and it leaves me deficient,
My voice box, too empty to yell.
I take love so serious, I try to invest,
Perchance they will hope for the same.
Yet every new friend means another failed test,
And my feelings will reveal my shame.

I can't afford to be let down again,
When I need help, I'm destined to fall.
Yet I lend to others, and sacrifice then,
The phone rings and you miss the call.
I need to know that I'm not alone,
Even a text would suffice.
I admit to my loneliness being self imposed,
Yet I always pay the same price.

Is honesty really that hard to comprehend,
Instead of just sounding demure?
I'd rather keep drowning, than have you pretend,
And give me emotions impure.
Parting is sorrow, yet lying is worse,
As I crash on the rocks down below.
Although you said different, I was never really first,
Put my mind at peace, let me go.

Afterthought: Here's another one for the brooding
hearts that are healing from broken relationships.
This is one of my favorite styles to write, as this
particular emotion is so common and empathetic.
The breakup poems here can be very cathartic and
freeing.

NO PLACE LIKE HOME:

I sit in the stillness, hearing the desolate hum of idle machinery, viewing very little difference from the images of my year long departure. The backgrounds and colors look to be supplanted in stability, while the faces are what flip around like revolving doors. My thoughts here have evolved, though the dreams of life, and hopes to be larger than that life, remain intact. I hope I'm just one of many to partake in the silent stillness of the empty theatre, and I pray for the same transformation in these unknown characters that I saw in myself in my 4 years of learning there. My name gets called through the halls like an infamous movie quote, which allows me the grandeur of knowing my social success. Moreover, the thoughts of the shows and people that passed through my experience ring out, into sayings, images, and days that will live on as long as those quiet theatre noises. I wish to you all a time never to be forgotten, with people and days as good as I had. They say you can't go home again, but though it will never be the same, you're never too far from that isolated contemplation.

Afterthought: This is one of the few pieces in which I talk about another big chapter of my life, theatre. I spent years at CCAC South directing, lighting, and running sound for shows there. Now I spend years going back there to act in them. This poem is my take on sitting in the empty theatre, returning to the building that made me so happy and confident.

EASY:

What IS easy?

Why does everyone long for easy?
Why does nothing ever come easy?
No matter how big or small our problem is, we can
never find it.
It's never around no matter how hard we hope or
pray.
Things in life haunt us everyday, and keep us awake
at night, and it's like easy doesn't exist. I'm here to
tell you why:

Easy is fun
Easy is quick
Easy is popular
Easy is desired
Easy is uneventful
but most of all, easy is...unrealistic

Easy is cowardice.
Easy is a cop out.
Easy is a lie.
Easy is a dream that will never come.
Easy is without any true test.
Easy keeps us from ever knowing what we can
handle.
Easy stops us from growing or forcing us to take
risks.
Easy holds us back, and keeps us marred in false
content.
Easy is the easy choice, but not always the right
one.
It's easy to quit and to give up, but to stand up and
fight for yourself, isn't so easy.

It's even easy for me to write this as I've created it,
but will I be able to back up these words and act on
them as I should? Only time will tell. But if I do, it

won't be easy.

Afterthought: This format is a lot different than most other poems you'll see in this book. But I've always liked the idea of hard work, of striving to be the best, and of conquering every obstacle you ever face. That drive and chip on my shoulder is what motivates this piece.

BACK TO TOMORROW:

It only takes a few crossed words,
to deflate a growing bond,
and so the time has dulled our shine,
like the moon over a pond.
I could never place the exact moment,
we lost touch and grew apart,
our sunny days turned gray with haze,
and hollowed out my heart.

I stare at this page and wonder,
is there anything I can do?
How did memories get lost with ease,
and block me from your view?
I spent the time to know you well,
and filled you with details,
and now you're empty and I'm just simply,
the breath that you exhaled.

Some boyfriend's gotten in the way,
or new friend, or maybe distance,
but part of me died with tears in my eyes,
when you erased my existence.
I need you more than ever now,
this effort's not in vain,
we shared the moments so please own it,

embrace my falling frame.

Please don't make our years seem wasted,
were we ever close at all?
This detoured road seems nearly closed,
I'm inches from the fall.
I understand I'm paranoid,
this has happened all before,
I've faced tragic ends with many friends,
but this one seemed so sure.

Just tell me that I'm silly now,
say it's all in my head,
from endless days to monthly breaks,
the signs pronounce us dead.
I won't forget our journey,
though this point must deplete,
I beg this you to be untrue,
I reel at your conceit.

For once I don't implicate myself,
insured my hands are clean,
and our glory days are stored away,
our moments kept pristine.
A smile washes over me,
as I romanticize your glance,
I dial your phone, so please be home,
this is our final chance...

Afterthought: This is one of my absolute favorites.
This is one of the few poems of mine that ends in a
"Schrodinger's Cat" scenario. I let my readers
choose their own ending based on their mood/frame
of mind. This piece articulates the black and white,
good and bad in all relationships.

144 HOURS:

That little green bear still sits in my closet, and
takes space in my memory every instance that I step
back for a momentary seat inside those Carolina
nights. Awkwardly stepping into the thought that
we tread the line of borrowed time, our hearts leapt
fearlessly into the 144 hours we had. The warships
targeted me on that July Saturday, but no shot
struck me as hard as the coast of your innocent
beauty. The stars in the sky had no chance against
the arcade in that moonlight. Not really
understanding the happenstance just makes the time
seem even more vivid, in a translucent sort of way.
I'll take the audible lies if it keeps my mind spotless
in the presence of your eyes. That way the past is all
encompassing. My relevance to your elegance is not
the passing stamp, but the scattered dream. The
nights seemed eternally extending, for that perfect
week. The lights on that arcade are off now, as off
as the writing on this page. The building nothing
more than a place to pump gas. But those 144 hours
will never be dimmed or changed beyond my mind.
That little green bear waits for his next escape in
whatever form it comes in.

Afterthought: As you can see by now, I love to
reminisce. There is a lot of talk about childhood and
innocence in this book. This is the purest form of
those ideas in this poem, a youthful crush. Crushes
seem so perfect and endless, especially as a child. I
doubt that girl is reading this right now, but you
never know.

THE BIRTH AND DEATH OF THE DAY:

Every step another wobble, there was no ground that could save me, I've been chained up by this slavery, but don't want to be a baby. Couldn't help but think that maybe, God was trying to page me, yet the pain was getting worse, and I was losing life daily. My neck burned like a fire, dousing my tranquility, and finally I felt like a kid with a disability.

I lost my normal smile as I marred in this depression, every good day surrounded by bad, as my heart felt regression. I forgot who I was, and didn't even want to know me, as some people sent good wishes, even others tried to show me. I tried to put on a false brave face and take it all in stride, but for the first time I knew I didn't want to be alive.

I no longer felt accepted, my loss of strength had left me dormant, so I turned to my friends constantly to make me feel important. I felt embarrassed needing help, so I kept friends elevated, and if something fell just slightly short then I got agitated. I want to say I'm sorry now, for being such a pest, I thought getting attention was some form of success.

When the wheelchair was the option, I was going with the flow, if I couldn't stand on my feet again, I told life I'd let go. Truth is I could have died, without any other choice, but somehow I beat the odds again, thanks to His rejoice.

But the surgery is over, now the road back has begun. I'll fight now more than ever because this battle's far from won. I still don't feel so special, nor

the need to impress, but this poem is my way of
exposing my open chest. You knew I had to talk
about it, to try and gain some clarity, I just hope you
all will feel this, exposed to my sincerity. I thank
you all for every visit, and your kind and loving
words, I'm back to being me again, now the candle's
all that burns.

I'm sorry for my bitterness, and for hiding my sweet
spirit, but you knew I'd come around again, just had
to find endearment. So now I finish getting better,
I'll be there in mere weeks, the love you've given as
motivation, tears rolling down my cheek. I focus
now on being me, my actions must amend, I now
see the love and the truth and the life, and that may
never end.

Afterthought: This health piece was written in 2010,
weeks after my spine surgery and neck fusion, when
I thought I'd never walk again (for the second time).
I was in a really dark and scary place at that time,
but I was starting to come out the other side. I
wanted to take you inside my mind during that
unsure time.

UNCONTESTED WINDS:

You awaken in the morning, consistency intact.
Not even knowing your growing impact.
Unwavering faith, life shining through.
I'd give anything to see things as you do.

Immeasurable help in such a short time.
The very burning passion that originates this rhyme.
I try to hide my weakness behind my shallow

brawn.
To not show how much has changed in me, since
you've come and gone.

I try to hide the truth inside,
keeping my heart closed.
To let you know what you mean to me,
risks my soul being exposed.

But then you up and leave again,
like it's another test.
What good is it to mold someone,
and not be around to see progress?

Absence makes the heart grow fonder,
but also makes it weaker.
As I sit trapped inside the same sad song,
just like a broken speaker

I'm left alone with memories,
feeling like an exclusion.
Wondering if it was ever real,
or just a hopeful illusion.

The door to a mans soul is his eyes,
those lines are often spoken.
To see the truth inside me now,
everything is broken.

The best AND worst things at the same time,
it happened so much faster.
You changed my life and then you leave,
you beautiful disaster.

Though it should never be taken back,
so my pain is deceased.

I'd do it all over again,
so those memories are at peace

I fight myself with feelings mixed,
over before it begins.
You just flow on and never stop,
like uncontested winds.

Afterthought: As a passenger of the Access system,
I come across all kinds of different interesting
characters. The same goes for being part of my
church, and my charity organization that I founded
in 2012 ("Causes For Hope"). I wanted to write a
piece about all the positive AND negative people
that come into your life for just a day, an hour, or a
few minutes, and how they can impact your mood.
They have journeys too, and it's beautiful how they
can affect yours.

NEVER SAY GOODBYE:

November 27th, 2011. Nothing ever really changes,
except the names of those beside you. You always
said I'd be a writer, so I guess I will abide you. A
year seems to pass like only a week in time. Some
things still linger with me, and I assume they always
will. The way you'd blast your out-of-style boom
box, playing some 80's music that nobody else
wanted to hear for the 100th time. How you loved
the rain, and would stop whatever you were doing
to sit outside and listen to it. So when it rained the
day you died, and the day of your funeral, I knew
better than to think it was just nature. You could've
fought much harder, before taking the plunge,
though I'll never understand it, it's not my place to
judge. I don't know why you gave up, but now

you're gone too soon, I miss your goofy sentences, I even miss your food. The smell of your chicken and rice still permeates my nose, and triggers the thoughts of how the kids on the block would come running for miles just to have some. I hearken back to all the pool parties and family gatherings, where you'd always be the loudest person, with a Milwaukee's Best in one hand and a 'Terrible Towel' in the other. I guess God could work it no other way than to have you protect me from above. Even on my strongest day, a tear falls from my eye, but the best thing you always taught me, was to never say goodbye. Cause I know somehow you're still here, in the traits that you've passed down, you've given me this confidence, so it's like YOU'RE writing now. So hold Heaven's gates wide open, or else I won't get in, I swear I'll keep on fighting, until we meet again. So I hope that you've enjoyed this, until God calls my name, I'll be looking at your picture, and waiting for the rain…

Afterthought: Finally we've come to the title piece of this adventure. My mother passed away in 2011, and I was very close to her. She was always the biggest supporter and advocate of me being a writer when I grew up. So it was only fitting that I dedicate this project to her and make this the centerpiece. Anyone who is going through losing a loved one, breathe. Take it one day at a time and remember, they want you to stay productive and positive, and they're always with you.

SURGICAL ROBBERY:

Why is it that bed is always ten times harder to get out of when you know you're going somewhere that you don't want to go? I know this morning I have to go to the doctor, and it's even more tragic today because the only appointment times that were available were before 7AM. I don't even think my alarm clock HAS a 7AM. But I have no other alternative but to go, because the office has sent me 12 confirmation e-mails and called me every day for the last week to remind me. So I arrive at the office nice and early to sign in as they told me to, just so I can sit here in the waiting room for the next 3 hours. The algorithm is simple. If your appointment is at 7, you get there at 6:30, and they'll get to you by about noon. Don't worry though, to pass the time, you get to pretend to read articles in magazines from 1984, in dead silence. For further satisfaction, you can look around at the pained expressions on others' faces as they try to avoid eye contact and pretend to look like they don't want to strangle the person next to them. Then you fill out paperwork that you've filled out 1,000 times before, just in case you've changed your middle initial or feel the need to finally confess your drinking habits. Finally they call your name, and now you think it's getting better. Not really though, because you now have to sit in the doctors office for another hour while he finishes his game of Angry Birds on his IPhone. He finally envelopes the doorway with his presence, and my muscles incumbently tighten, because no matter how old I am, I will always scream at the sight of needles or blood. Random thought: why can't the cute female nurse be the one to grab your balls and tell you to cough instead of the creepy old guy with the hump? Anyway…the actual physical itself only takes about 4 minutes. So glad this cost me $87. But before I go, I must schedule another appointment so I can return to this sweet hell all over again in 6 months. I think I'm busy that day.

Afterthought: After the last several poems were so heavy, I figured I'd lighten the mood with a poem from my stand-up comedy series. Nobody likes going to the doctor, and I've been there enough days to last me a lifetime. So why not poke some fun at the entire ridiculous process.

PEELING BACK THE VEIL:

Did you ever get the feeling that you could look into a mirror without having to pose in front of glass? That without ever REALLY knowing someone, you've still experienced their life story. That feeling can be one of the most powerful in creation when the person you're peering into accepts the reciprocal, but all the more disappointing, when you're exposing a veil they've yet to lift. I don't mean to stir, but this half closed door is open just enough to have me caught in between. I may not know you well, but I know enough, because the mask you wear to fight off the scars was taken from my own closet. So I'll fit whatever role it takes to pacify this moment, for shouting the truth would only frighten away the possibilities. But know that our raindrops are crashing together, and I ache inside, having to watch it continue to fall. Time is but a myriad of seconds, run together, wasted never saying what would save and free us all. Save us all that next contusion and please peel that veil, before it becomes too hazy to see the other side.

Afterthought: We all have at least that one person in our lives, whether best friend or relative or spouse, that we feel is the exact same person as we are.

When there's a rift in that relationship, it makes you question how correct you were. So this one goes out to all of the mirror images of us out there. May you always remember that you love that person, because you and them and one in the same.

3AM:

I lay awake restlessly, as I turn in my bed,
the eerie still and silence deafen me.
The ideas of being used, infiltrate my head,
and yet I'm still the very last to see.

These memories are haunting, I must leave them alone,
too many times I'm buried at your knees.
Yet every time you call, I instantly answer the phone,
I never grasp the forest through the trees.

But I cannot be your 3AM, can't be your last resort,
I can't be the one to catch you when you fall.
The stronger me's not settling, I'm blind to your retort,
I'm losing you but gaining back it all.

I've learned a lesson, paid the cost, not at your beckon call.
My head can now resist manipulation.
I've extricated you from me, and now I'm standing tall,
that once fascinated me, now not temptation.

Because I cannot be your 3AM, can't be your backup plan,

can't be a shadow lurking on the side.
The ego-stroking days are over, go hunt another man,
I'm losing you but gaining back my pride.

You took us for granted, played upon emotion,
and used our history to benefit,
You misread my kindness, for unwavering devotion,
and made our memories irrelevant.

Once more I cannot be your 3AM, can't be your childish game,
all my foolish nights I now amend.
What was once a burning fire, is now merely a flame,
my phone no longer rings at 3AM.

Afterthought: This is one of my favorites in this book, because it's empowering. I've talked a bit about failed friendships in here, and this one speaks to those people that only talk to you when they need you. This is a shout back at those greedy people who use you at their convenience. Always know your worth, and only give of yourself to those who are willing to give to you as well.

STARRY NIGHT:

People continue to stare at us, gawking at the amazing colors, or the detailed imagery, yet never really knowing what they're looking at. They'll never understand the magnitude of this moment, the change that their eyes will undergo upon viewing us, they just know what they've heard all along, that this is a masterpiece. Our stars are lit to protect the world, to oversee its proceedings, and to ask that our light shines through the windows of those that pray for hope. Our burning bulbs are meant to hang suspended forever, to show the world what perfection is supposed to look like. It doesn't matter what museum we are moved to, or how many times we're painted over, all that matters is that we're here to illuminate even the darkest night, and that our image never changes. God was our Vincent Van Gogh, and his brush stroked our canvas to blend us for a reason. Evolution causes tides to rip, houses to crumble, and trees to sway, yet our stars stay put, waiting for the next chance to save humanity from the night. So alter what you will, but our flashing bulbs guide this town either way, standing tall for all who will gaze into us.

Afterthought: I have quite the love for physical art, just as I do for written art, but I was never blessed with the gifts to draw or paint. Van Gogh's "Starry Night" is perhaps my favorite painting ever, so this is my homage to it. I compare it here to some of my favorite relationships, drama free and a model of positive energy.

THIS TATTERED BRIDGE:

I'm standing on a bridge. There are two potential outcomes in front of me. Off the easy way or the hard way. The easy way is the way out. The drop below can seem like nothing in comparison to the trying life ahead. Just a simple closing of the eyes and forward step, and all the perils of the past and stress over my head are forgotten. The hard way entails the step back. Back to reality, back to struggle, back to the life I never thought I'd live. They say life flashes before your eyes right before you die, but it really flashes right before the biggest moments you live. There I see every misstep, every letdown, every time I reached up to touch bottom, and every time I became the antithesis of someone's otherwise serendipitous existence. I advance to take that step, and my successes somehow force-field me. That same manifest of failures is the motivation to do better. I take a step back and breathe deeply, and choose life, simply because love is stronger than hate. My pangs make me stronger, and my crises make me wiser. I have more in my life than this tattered bridge, more than I ever saw before, and I hope the next person at this bridge can draw the same conclusion.

Afterthought: This is a modification of a poem that I wrote for an English class contest in high school. I've always loved the idea of a grappling battle between good and evil, or any difficult choices in life. Everyone comes to a bridge in their lives at some point, or another metaphorical fork in the road. Life always goes on, no matter how dark the night before may seem.

HOMEMADE ARCADE:

The first thing you notice is how the mornings start getting lighter in the spring. The air felt different back then…sweeter, vernorexic. School didn't seem like a job at all, it was something we looked forward to. We used to show up at the crack of dawn, not like I had a choice. My mom had to get there early so she could start her prep work, popping toast in the toaster and covering herself in her dingy red DCS uniform. Those 127 steps from home to school were filled with wonder for us, because the San Francisco 49ers had a world championship to win. After our football triumph, and knocking the cinnamon for the toast all over the floor, it was time to see how many breakfast pizzas or sausage biscuits I could get my mom to buy me. I'm surprised I wasn't 300 pounds. Next we voyage upstairs so we could rap the new verse from the song we just learned 40 times in a row until our friends notice. After that, we either slept on our desks or wrestled as sneakily as possible while our teacher read some book about war. But the best part of the day was when gang-warfare broke out. Anytime they sent us to the boiler room to store things away, we took the opportunity to try out our favorite wrestling moves on each other, and used our mental diagrams of the school to get the advantage. Not sure we ever settled who was the best group...D-Next, Wicked Clowns, or Dog-Pound? After stealing some carefully planned notes out of the girls desks (sorry 8th graders!), it was time to go home and plan how we'd win the next battle tomorrow while we sat on the swing. I look at that building now, defunct and decrepit, and I wonder how the clock could race so rapidly. If those walls could talk, I think we'd all still be in detention.

Afterthought: This one will be a confusing read for most people. I wanted to create a grade school piece recalling a lot of the silly inside jokes and secret journeys we had back then. I'm so lucky to still be friends with so many of those people, and it was one of the best times of my life. Sorry for all the personal references here, but I hope you can all appreciate the joys of being so young and careless and remembering your past.

THE MAN WHO WOULDN'T MOVE:

As the background changes and leaves will fall,
I'll be standing still with you through it all,
I'll never leave.
As the people pass aimlessly on the street,
and you search for the ground holding up your feet,
tt will be me.

As the rear-view grows and the present fades,
and the chores mount up near the end of days,
keep holding on.
When the window cracks, pillars fall apart,
but I'll be your light keeping out the dark,
to keep you strong.

Life has this way to wear us down,
but my arms will be your stable ground
It's not the end.
You gaze out the window to slow the plight,
block out tomorrow, breathe in tonight,
then try again.

No matter what others invade our lives,
what's here is different, we see the signs,
it's beyond verbs.
As one grows older, perceptions switch,
but the winds of change won't move me an inch,
there are no words.

So smell the flowers, run through the fields,
pull up a seat on a beach-front pier,
and start anew.
So grow your wings out and take a look,

at the beauty waiting in every nook,
it's all for you.

Afterthought: This was a late addition, and a newer
piece I'd written. I've always tried to pride myself
on being a kind-hearted friend who was there
through a lot of others' hard times. Sometimes the
most comforting thing out there is to know that
someone has your back, and will do all they can for
you in any circumstance. To any readers of this
book, friend, family, or poetry enthusiast, I am here
to be a shoulder and an ear, any time you may need
one.

THIS CLOUD:

You try and turn away, but I can see it in your eyes,
the reality is stirring in my soul.
But lets avoid the truth because I'd rather hear the
lies,
tt hurts less when I try and play the fool.
I refuse to see tomorrow, I'm just living in tonight,
denial is the best of my defenses.
I'm holding up the walls and I'm clinging to the
fight,
because yesterday is keeping me dependent.

Just pretend that we're okay, that we'll make it
through the day,
I know I'm dreaming and screaming out loud.
I have illusion to believe that connections are
retrieved,
just let me float around on this cloud.

So now you're all excited, that you've found
somebody new,

and although I want to yell, I stay refined.
I should be elated for you, but I can't help feeling
blue,
as memories create unrest inside my mind.
My tongue feels like a fire, with the words all
trapped inside,
and I see that nothing's like it was before.
You've lost your will to hold me, so I'm choosing
to stay blind,
I'm on this cloud, while you're heading for the
door.

Just pretend that we're alright, that we'll make it
through tonight,
your veil and wedding dress are hanging like a
gown.
So though you're moving on, those perfect nights
are far from gone,
as I'm laying here alone up on this cloud.

Tell me to be contrite, that we'll make it through
this life,
I'm at your grave, but I know you're looking down.
Though life tore us apart, you will always have my
heart,
maybe now we can finally share this cloud.

Afterthought: This is a rather sad piece, but I felt
that I needed to share it. It centers around the denial
of a one-sided relationship, where one person
always changes and makes excuses for the other. I
went further to explore one person holding on
through the others' stages of life. You can't help
who you love, and sometimes that can be a sad
thing, because it closes doors on other
opportunities.

MIRAGE

I turn my head with every fiber in my being, I must avoid your eyes one final time. Can't bear to look at you and see another foolish example of how I gave in. What I once longed for so deeply, is now the one thing that would break me into pieces. I pray to God my phone stays quiet in this sleepless night, for the noise would simply equate another regression. We always lived on borrowed time, as any two unequals do, but the final cast stone wasn't even worth the throw. There's no use to harbor the ship, for that only means waiting for the next wave to pull me deeper. Then I think about the years we've beheld, and slowly they begin to fade, like the pages of a tattered novel to which we've forgotten the outcome. You've landed the biggest blow by doing nothing at all, now please do me the same courtesy of keeping that consistent. You hold out your hands like the next rock on a mountain, only making the fall more severe when they give out again. Though I'd rather take this crash in peace than to hit more pointed rocks below. I'd say my heart is broken, but that's a mere euphemism, for my heart is so translucent it can no longer be touched. So stay back, keep true, I want to understand this puzzle. I go to speak this last goodnight to you, and as I look into your eyes, praying to see coldness. I'm talking to myself, and you were never there at all.

Afterthought: Another from the Myrtle Beach series. This one is fairly self-explanatory, examining a relationship where you see something completely the opposite of how it actually is.

IN DREAMS:

People walk the halls everyday, and I walk them just as fervently, as if to blend in with the crowd. Nobody gets too close, for the wall I've spent decades building would just send them crashing in a heap to the floor. When I see you, you get the same reaction, so as not to trigger the alarms in your head. I'll keep preaching my addendum as if it's on a loop, bantering to a fault that romantic love is a sham and relationships aren't for anybody, pandering to all that will listen that my heart has gone cold and there's no room for girls in my crowded manifest. But in dreams, I can escape that harsh reality and run freely with you. We can escape into the ocean with nothing but the teal blue skies looking down. In dreams, there's no room for my tiring speeches, because all I have time for is the depth of your eyes. My head's given way, and my heart is free-falling, and I wouldn't dare to slow it down, in dreams. Back in reality, I don't make the list of any of the qualities you desire, and there's nothing I can do to change that. All I can do is gaze on as you settle for guys who will clearly fall short, as tears in your eyes punch holes in my soul again. Your painted personality and energy fill me up, but your honesty is harsher than daggers. I dash home to sleep, for Shakespeare had it right, inside those eyelids lay a chance at the unthinkable. In dreams, I'd catch your falling hopes and cherish them everyday. In dreams, I'd be a better man, and could speak with lips that make everyday a mystery for you instead of a chore. I'd make up for all I'm missing, and we could hide from the world, as our circadian lives only need each other. So I'll keep coping on rejection, in hopes that one day these words pierce your ears, in dreams.

Afterthought: Rejection is something we've all dealt with, and I wanted to include that unified theme in this book. Most people also use defense mechanisms in coping, or have two conflicting sides to how they choose to deal with people. So I present the yin and yang of hopeless romantics, who cut themselves off from possibilities due to the reality of rejection.

WAITING FOR THE MEMORIES:

You go from 25 to 12 in seconds, every time you reminisce. For every bill that haunts you today, you saw 10 more sunsets you can never take back. Every business meeting is usurped by a SNICK or TGIF TV show, and every college class or internship finds it's way back to a pick-up basketball game, through the caverns of your mind. Your body knows no limits of the pain that surrounds it today. Your heart doesn't feel the spikes of loves embrace, but only the excitement of another eternal night. Girls didn't exist as they do now, credit cards were baseball cards, cell phones were screams from up the street, and wallets were pockets that contained a $10 bill you conned your dad into. I lay awake at 12 years old, not thinking of how scary the future would be, but how cool the present was. I sneak downstairs for a glimpse at the cake in the fridge, not looking for another mess to clean or script to write. The good outweighs the bad, age never increases, and our hearts were too short-sighted to be jaded. Now those summers move on, the days go by faster than speeding trains, and life has become a term we see with the eyes of cynicism. Yet still, as the drawbridge raises up with finality, you can never steal away what's embedded inside. And your mind rests, waiting, for another chance to open up to the journey that got us here. So as those grown up activities pile up and stress piles on, your mind's still waiting, to relive what lasts forever. Breathe in, step back, it's waiting.

Afterthought: This is from the workshop series, and is another happy glance at childhood. On the tireless days when adulthood seems too much to bare, I like to reread these types of poems and recall that memories last forever.

BLAMING MYSELF:

From the start it seemed wrong, as I stepped to the top.
I had others around me, but the pain never stopped.
For those that got out from under my life so hallow.
Which was harmful enough, and worse yet did fallow.
To have your life saved, changed and protected,
but then get abandoned by those most affected.
Mere words can't compare, they fail to describe,
that truest emotion, that fleeting inside.
I don't reflect drama, that's not my intention.
It's just not in my dimensions to make an impression.
It happens to many, some can't be blamed of,
but how is your legacy one you're ashamed of?
As happy as I am, I can't fight the sensation,
that it falls back on me, it's my condemnation.
So for now this gets buried, back on the shelf,
in the end there is no one to blame but myself.

Afterthought: Nobody is perfect, we all make mistakes. Admitting that is the first step to getting over it. You have to forgive yourself and clear your conscience before others can forgive you. Don't hold on to bad decisions, make peace with them.

THE GUY BEHIND THE KEYBOARD:

Getting out of bed might be the hardest part of the whole day. Every single day, I make a conscious choice. I can either stay in bed and let my fleeting body shut itself down, or fight with all I have to pull myself up through the pain to try and make an impact for one more day. I always choose the latter, no matter how much physical pain that choice entails. Everyone has a story, but mine is more like a badge of honor. From the minute I walk out the door I've got a million eyes on me. Some feel sympathy, some just wonder, and some just laugh. No reaction ever bothered me though, you'll never catch me with my head down in a hallway. Being born with cerebral palsy is one thing, because you're too young to understand what's going on. I was told I'd never be born, but I was. I was told I'd never walk, but I did. I was told I'd never be able to learn mentally, or function socially. Yet here I am, a college graduate and a published author. A self-sufficient homeowner with more blessings and love than one person could ask for. And then in 2010, a herniated disc struck my spine, and made the cerebral palsy worse than ever before. To beat all the odds and overcome a condition is a joyous miracle, but to then come back after 23 years and have things taken away from you again, is indescribable. So I lost balance control and was no longer able to do the athletic things I loved. But again, you'll never hear me complain. God always gives us far more than he takes away. When asked "what's the hardest part about growing up with Cerebral Palsy?", the psychological part is always my answer. I can deal with the pain, because I'm a fighter. I can deal with the stares of the uninformed, because I wish to educate them instead of scold them. I can deal with the stereotypes, because I want to positively represent everyone that has CP, every time I step outside my front door. I want to show kids that have what I have, that they can do and be, ANYTHING they want to be. It's hard having the mind of a 28 year old and the body of a 70 year old, and seeing yourself regress, that's the real challenge. But I will keep walking down the street with my head up, smiling, and kicking this disabilities ass, with every breath I have left. Give God the glory, and know you never lose unless you stop fighting.

Afterthought: This one really isn't as much a poem as it is a statement. This was a late addition, and it doesn't really have any flow or sequence. But poetry is always better if you can relate to it, so I wanted to give you a glimpse into the author you're reading. I just want to let anybody out there with a disability know that you are loved, you are strong, and you can overcome anything. Never let someone else tell you what you can't do. With hard work and faith, you can change the world. You ARE changing the world.

FOOTPRINTS IN THE SAND:

Step one was all excitement, ideas were fresh intact,

we never had to plan for what's in store.
Time was not constricting, fun was the only pact,
our future seemed as open as the shore.

Step five got a little hotter as connections got
stronger,
light treading did endow as we got near.
Then we continued to grow closer, strides became a
little longer,
the sand between our toes abandons fear.

Step ten may be the scariest, because then you can't
turn back,
we got past the point of no return.
These hearts are feeling risky, but we heard the
waves on track,
now we must endure the searing burn.

Step twenty leaped intensity, our journey became
rough,
all our pleasant steps turned to emotion.
Always keeping perfect footprints is really proven
tough,
we thought we'd never make it to the ocean.

Step forty then reminded me, I loved our
destination,
the water was too near to stop the fight.
So we formulated prints again with further
penetration,
and off we went again to find the light.

Step fifty went right to a ditch, we crashed along
some shells,
even feet away, we had to stop.
You can't complete a duo's journey when thinking

of yourselves,
the tide becomes so high, it has to drop.

The seashell that she once gave me, was thrown
back into the waves,
those steps from yesteryear have failed today.
Now those that walk the sands are just visiting our
graves,
as our footprints in the sand got washed away.

Afterthought: Can you tell this one was written at
the beach? I love larger than life comparisons, and
this piece really struck me as being strong. I
compare that exciting and scary journey from the
beach into the water to a rocky, unsure relationship.
It ends on a sad note, but of course, it doesn't have
to. Sometimes those footprints can't ever be fully
erased.

MAP BACK TO HOME:

Too many times, too many lies,
that left me dead and broken.
I found myself lost, marred in disguise,
penalized for being outspoken.
I blamed myself, and then the world,
in dealing with rejection.
Not knowing the plan that God unfurled,
I failed to seek perfection.

Your heart can take so many blows,
before it comes undone.
But it must be cold before it snows,
and then you see the sun.
I sat in darkness on the ledge,
had all I could withstand.

Then your light shone through and pulled me off the edge,
at the end it all began.

I was proven wrong to expect the worst,
you came and saved my spirit.
For the first time I finally finished first,
and you raised my ears to hear it.
And when I'm down, you bare my cross,
and I no longer feel alone.
Now I gaze at you when I'm feeling lost,
and your eyes are my map back to home.

Like a child now I dance around,
as these clichés cause the jealous to stare.
And your innocent beauty aspires to astound,
yet the key is that you're unaware.
It's the complete package of total attraction,
that keeps my brood light in it's tone.
You keep my hand steady with every infraction,
and your heart is my map back to home.

Afterthought: I'm a sucker for a good Nicholas Sparks style love poem declaration. It's amazing how the right person can just motivate you to be better, and change your outlook on every aspect of life. You must appreciate those people every day, and never forget to tell them how they've helped you.

YOUR SINKING SHIP:

He received the call early that morning,
the tone of their voices provided the warning.
Another had passed on and left us in mourning.
The casket was closing, the spirit deporting.

With the young ones behind, strength must come
from within,
but with your own life in limbo, how could freedom
begin?
Immortality weakens as you give in to sin,
how could anyone face death and possibly win?

I've had your back now time and time again,
but when I held you close, you let me slip.
We're repeating hateful words as icebergs crash,
it's time for me to jump off your sinking ship.

The next few days were the toughest ever,
his tears clinched tight, his words still clever.
Yet the one who's closest pulled the lever,
and made this issue a bigger endeavor.
She made light of the situation,
with hurtful words that caused frustration.
As he lost family and faced aggravation,
she sat there stoic with condemnation.

I'm tired of all the times you let me down,
every other step's another trip,
the waves with us are in over our heads now,
it's time for me to leave your sinking ship.

He staggered to the phone to take a call,
and was told that yet again he's bound to fall.
These doctors scared, their back against a wall,
tell me I will probably lose it all.
Where can you turn when your heart is busted?
This life can leave you maladjusted.
You wait for the news as your heart hits percussion,
as those around you mock, disgusted.

I'm sick of letting your words bring me down,
I was once your whole world, now I'm just a blip.
As I'm headed for that latest fatal rock,
it's time for me to drown your sinking ship.

Afterthought: So here's the exact opposite of the
last poem I featured. Just as you must hold on to
those positive people, you must let go of the
negative ones. No matter how much you love
someone, they can be toxic to your life, and will
bring you down with them. This piece was also a
chance to show off a new form of rhyming couplets.

THE LIFE INSIDE THE MIRROR:

To begin with, breathe. Early and often. First and
last. The world will not change and evolve over
you, but through you. The day is never too much,
and the memories are never enough. Complacency
is the devil incarnate, failure is never final and
courage is the light that shines in the final hour
before the most important step. Let your heart be
wider than your ego, and your dreams be bigger
than the reasons you have not to achieve them. Stop
and see the beauty, for moments in time ring louder
than any bigger picture or any broken bridge. See
yourself in the golden mirror, and evoke that
reflection to all who dare to partake in its mystery.
That mirror will glow forever as time goes by, and
only you will dream to be the figure in it's
improvement. Be the breath that the world takes to
escape from it's own peril.

Afterthought: The inspiration for this poem came
from a workshop, where I was asked to write about
what advice I'd give to my child, if I had one.

INCEPTION:

I once thought I saved a girl on 1750 Clairton Road. She wasn't REALLY a ghost, but nobody else could ever see her the way that I did. Our journey began as most do at that address, embracing talent on a stage. It's funny how you can peer into somebody's soul before ever speaking a word to them. She tried to do with me what she did with everyone else, staying in character behind the curtain, hiding her heart behind walls of expectancy. But walls fall short when mirrors find each other. It was a day like any other when I finally broke through, when the reflection finally blinded her so deeply that she was forced to see. It was like "Inception", just... not as confusing. You'd think a bond like that would last forever, but 11 months later, forever came and went in a day. I screamed her name, from as high as I could, but all I heard in return was my own petulant echo. In seeing that mirror, I'd finally met someone who'd no longer cater to my stubborn rubric, so the calls stopped as quickly as they'd began. I felt akin to a horse with a bad leg, two actually, whose usefulness had met its end, and was being shot because it was no longer needed. To hear from others about how brightly that mirror shines, after you've invested so much in it's luminosity, is a crime that's only penance is a broken heart. Eventually everyone finds their unequal, the hard part is seeing them be equal to everyone except you. You had to expect acting from a friendship born on a stage, right? So now I sit at 1750 Clairton Road, looking in the mirror, but no one's looking back at me. They never were. Now I awaken, realizing I've done inception on myself all along.

Afterthought: I love the opportunity to throw little bonuses in my writing, including homages of my other poems. In this piece, you'll notice a ton of references to poems you've already read (if you're reading this book in order). That's a way of me hinting at some of these subjects being linked, and some of the characters being together. As I said earlier, not everyone can (or wants to) be saved. It's more important to save yourself instead of being stressed and tortured.

ALWAYS AND FOREVER:

Throughout the years of any memorable life, stands a person beside that life, inside that life, to make it stand up. Quantifying your impact on my dusty pages in words would be the definition of injustice. I'm terribly awestruck at how God has woven you so tightly into my life, that our constant interaction still never grows tiresome, and how you accept my compulsion and protection, which only makes me strive to be better. We, together, have gone far beyond love, in such a way that renders timeless love stories helpless to compete with us. I melt inside your smile as our comfort ability lends its kind escape from the fears of life. I fade into your eyes as if to know there's another 'me' out there, one who elates at my every success and steadies my hand at every wrong turn. My former 'paranoia' as you called it, now just serves as assurance that the world stands still and watches us, as we carve our names in the record books, both by ourselves, and together. Every adorning room is put on pause as our coupled charisma lights up the faces of people who pass through our lives. Our inside jokes become the lifeline we need as all those around us fall. You provide a brief respite from my intense beliefs of destiny or that love doesn't exist, and I'd like to think my words have served as windows that deflected your tears. Forever means forever, and I'm lucky beyond emotion for every day, good and bad, we've ever had. Always is absolute, and we have promises to keep. 35 may seem to be light-years away, but keep your spirit sweet, because time goes fast, and these broken legs have bridges that you need to help me cross. This isn't just a phase, or a wave that dies down with the passing of time. So take these friendly thoughts and know your affect, on me, and everyone you grace with the opportunity to know you. You may not have a halo, but what you have is far greater, for it is enough to bring these words to life and truth. Continue to keep your skies clear, because I'm ready to stand next to you in the stars. Always and Forever.

Afterthought: This is another piece of mine that was written specifically for one person. She always wanted a poem of mine to herself, but I'm so blessed that she allowed me to share this with the world, because I'm very proud of this. It's not often that you get to share your true feelings with one of your best friends, and have it forever written in the world, before it's too late. Her friendship has been one of the closest and truest loves I've ever had the privilege of feeling. Always…

SOUTH SIDE SYNDROME:

When I get the call around 5PM on a Saturday afternoon, it can only mean one thing: a select group of friends are trying to gather the troops for an evening on Carson Street. My friends think that picking up girls is the same as picking out underwear at Target. I never understood why it takes guys about 20 minutes to get ready, while it takes girls about 20 days. So we put on our best clothes and pretend we're not poor, in hopes of finding that special someone, even though girls only go to clubs to tease guys anyway. So we walk for what feels like 17 miles, all in the hopes that some girl who's had too many apple-tini's will stagger into us. So we amble in, and see a group of girls right away. But every group has that one girl that you have to impress in order to gain access to the others. The one who determines if you're allowed to talk to her friends. The leader of the pack. We call her the prude patrol. Or the guardian of the gate. So we approach smoothly, like a slinky, counting each step out loud so we don't appear to be drunk. I notice that some of the pumps you ladies try to fit your feet into, make it appear like Darth Vader has your toes in a death grip. The mere thought of them hurts my feet. It sucks that when guys drink beer, they have to pee four times an hour. So I waddle to the bathroom and pick a stall so that I can pee like a 4 year old boy, pants down, boxers down, ass naked to the world. Ah, heaven. But someone comes pounding on the door, and the first thought that comes to my alcohol-induced mind is…"it's the police. They're going to arrest me for peeing like a little boy. And I didn't even know that was a crime. The worst part is, I'm going to jail naked. That's like easy access for prisoners."

Afterthought: One final comedic piece to lighten the mood here. I've had so many classic nights with my friends in the South Side, so I figured I should immortalize it with some jokes. The stereotypes in the clubs really do hold true, even today. Go out and watch people sometime, it's one of the most hysterical things you can do.

LYRICAL DIVINITY:

All we're feeling now is the weight of the day.
And I ask the Holy Spirit to come and push it away.
The world's falling down like a weight on our backs.
And when the doubt creeps in then the devil attacks.
Then tacks are in our backs and we never relax.
The impact of the world's got us packed to the max.
So the soul gets weak and temptations pay a visit.
And we start giving in to trepidation so malicious.
The murders on TV got us trapped inside insanity.
Because we've lost sight, keep modesty over vanity.
They're foreclosing houses, everybody's got a rival.
People dying every day just fighting for survival.
So we start losing hope but I'm trying to rap.
About how this is God's world so we're taking it back.
So it's time for our pride to come out from inside.
So no reason to hide cause the fight is alive.
Let's stand up and use our energy to make a difference.
Because our crew runs deeper and they call us Christians.
So we're called to provide and to take it in stride.
Because Jesus Christ died just to keep us alive.
Gotta rise above hate, and don't be nipped by the serpents.
It's the hearts and the spirits that will rise to the surface.

God thank you for these words as I stand in
serenity.
There's no hate in these hearts, just lyrical divinity.

Afterthought: Since this book is a peak into my soul
and personality, I found it only fitting to include
another Christian poem here towards the end. I
don't want to force beliefs onto others or beat my
readers over the head with my faith, but it is an
important part of who I am. So if any of you would
like to hear my testimony or stories of why I'm a
devout Christian, feel free to ask. Always believe in
something, and stand up for it.

CAROLINA:

Your eyes,
where my future seemed comprised,
those days we'd just lay here together in a perfect
paradise.
Your smile,
where I'd get lost for a while,
my lonely heart got resurrected when you picked it
from the pile.

My days...,
before you feel erased,
my imperfections felt so perfect in your momentary
grace.
With time,
you made me feel alive,
so I started unveiling sentiments I used to hold
inside.

And it felt like Carolina, a lifetime on the beach,
our two souls intertwining, while waves crashed

across the sea.
Your sunshine hit me daily, like the sand between my toes,
but then things started changing, little did I know.

Your eyes,
a cavalcade of lies,
suddenly it became so clear, I saw through your disguise.
Your smile,
once fooled me for a while,
now I just feel defiled as you're acting like a child.

Intense,
why'd I come to your defense?
your actions now lay on an axis, we can never make amends.
These days,
the clouds have fallen gray,
I'm feeling blue cause I kept you, but threw myself away.

Now I escape to Carolina, running till I can't,
I'm hoping they can't find me, buried in the sand.
It was raining on me daily, the waves just had me thrown,
but then things started changing, little did I know.

My eyes,
so perfect and so wide,
I started seeing all my beauty, passion, love and pride.
My world,
unaffected by some girl,
every bright day lays ahead, as I surf another curl...

Now I'm back in Carolina, sitting near the shore,
I Parasail above the world, with tons of plans in store.
I hear the wind and see umbrellas, and see towels start to blow,
now nothing good in my life changes, and now I finally know.

Afterthought: This is the final piece of the Myrtle collection. It's also another attempt at a different style of verse. The most powerful thing about getting away is that it puts everything in perspective and makes your worries feel very small. No matter what range of emotions you go through, somebody out there always has it worse. How you choose deal with problems is far more important than the problems themselves.

INNOCENCE:

What do you think of, when you romanticize back into the innocence of your childhood? The days were fun, but the nights were endless. As the illuminated leaves begin to trickle from the trees, and the nights sky falls before the evening news, the careless gaggle of children run to ask their parents if their 10 best friends can spend the night. The countless colors of Fall fill the tiny suburban towns. The kids run free in the streets, going door to door in their creative costumes, asking for candy to fill their garbage bags. They didn't need escorts watching over them, and they didn't need to check all the candy when they got home. Everybody was safe, the town watched over itself. Nobody was online, we didn't even know what that was. We were all outside, tossing a football, discussing which Power Ranger was the coolest. C'mon guys, everyone knows it was Tommy. Nobody had their faces buried in their cell phones. If you wanted to see someone, you walked to his house and yelled outside his window. If you had a crush, you didn't Tweet her or poke her on Facebook, you poked her in real life, with a stick, while telling her she was gross, because your friends would make fun of you if they knew you liked someone. We just wanted to go to Kennywood in our hoodies and run around for hours. Credit cards, bills, taxes and jobs were just words our parents used when they wanted to bore us to sleep. College was light-years away, heck, so was high school. All we could picture was making forts and helping Mario save the Princess. We didn't need cars or insurance, we had our personal chauffeurs, AKA mom and dad, take us everywhere. Healthcare wasn't important because we had band-aid's, and two more hours until they called us in. So before the snow begins to lay where our leaves and lawns used to, look outside the window one more time, and see yourself running into the sunset. No matter what happens after, nothing can ever catch you.

Afterthought: This poem is pretty similar to a few of the others in the childhood collection, but I wanted something like this towards the end of this book. Youth is immortal, because nobody can ever take away what you've done. If you take nothing else away from this book, then at least BE HAPPY. Happiness is the key to life. We only get one.

SWAN SONG:

There come single days in every man's life,
when he says what he's wanted to say.
And although the result will cut like a knife,
these words hide temptation away.

Their rise was meteoric, in such swift proportions,
their closeness was merely unmatched.
But intensified feelings could cause such distortions
and render their future detached.

I kept it platonic and loved from afar,
yet I knew that I trailed from the start.
My intentions remained but my head came ajar,
though I still tried to hijack my heart.

I locked truth away and denied from myself,
the connection that made all this happen.
This one stood out from my previous wealth,
and made my old attitude flatten.

Don't be mistaken, I remained realistic,
this beauty was too good for me.
She was out of my league, to be more simplistic,
that perfection's what kept me intrigued.

But it's time to let go, no use to hold on,
to a dream that was never achieved.
And I have no hard feelings, to blame you is wrong,
so I will confess, then concede.

So this is our swan song, our coda, our end,
the concluding act of our show.
Our bond is still timeless, we'll always be friends,
but as more, I will finally let go.

Afterthought: This is my favorite poem I've ever

written to date. Although it has some sad overtones, I truly find it to be the purest love poem in this book, because it's about the love of two best friends. Whether that love culminates in taking the chance at romance, or just remaining as close as friends can be, that is beautiful and unalterable. Never be afraid to love as hard as you can. To love and be loved, is the reason we're here. Which is a great segue into my final piece in this journey…

MANIFEST:

Love; give it openly, freely, and without compensation. Also allow yourself to receive it, and know you always deserve it. Never settle. Don't let someone take you for granted, no matter what the objective. Don't push people away, for one day they'll get tired of pushing back. Never do anything in the heat of the moment; while it will feel great for 5 minutes, it will make you feel terrible for the next 6 months. Stop and enjoy everything you do; never work so hard that you don't get to appreciate what you're working for. Put yourself in someone else's mirror before casting judgment on it's reflection. Money is a means to an end, not a reason for living. Use it to fill necessities and to help others, not to satiate your own gluttony. What you do as an occupation, what you drive for transportation, and where you live will NEVER be as important as who you are as a person. We are all judged on our works, not our material possessions. Don't have your face so buried in your technology that you can't encompass the beauty all around you. Furthermore, use your technology to edify yourself, not to simply pretend you're popular. Find time for the things that you love, as life is about happiness.

Always keep your ear to the pages of someone's story, for you never know how they fit into your book. The best nights you will have in your life are the ones you didn't spend a dollar on. Do nothing in fear, do it instead out of love for yourself. Never be afraid of life, nor death. We have to be in control of life, not letting it control us. And death...nobody can control. Be honest, brutally so. Tell people what they mean to you every chance you get...because you only get so many chances. Make mistakes, it's the only way to learn or improve. Dream as big as you can, to an insane extent...nobody sane or comfortable ever changed the world. Make an impact on everyone you come across, our legacy is all we leave behind. Give back, because what you gave away always means more than what you've kept. None of our gifts or abilities are ever fully because of us. Don't chase anything, work for something and watch as it unfolds. Respect other people, even strangers...we're all we have in this dangerous world. And lastly, love and be loved. Yes, I said it twice because it's the most important thing on the list.

Afterthought: I wanted this to be the final piece in the book, because it encompasses all the important things I've learned so far in my 28 years of life. It ends on a happy note, as all stories should. I've embraced my role as a life coach for many of my friends, and this is my chance to spread some of those tidbits of wisdom to whomever is turning these pages. I ask that you please read this poem most often of all, as we all need these reminders as often as we can get them. So this ends our journey together, for now. To anyone that has read this, I thank you all again, SO much, my valued readers and supporters. Every one of you has touched my life beyond words. I love you. Until we meet again…

Made in the USA
San Bernardino, CA
04 May 2015